The Itty-Bitty Icky Committee

Written by Debbie Lindsay

Illustrated by Francois Lange

I dedicate this book to my family, friends and clients for they have been my greatest teachers.

Balboa Press books may be ordered through booksellers or by contacting:

Balboa Press
A Division of Hay House
1663 Liberty Drive
Bloomington, IN 47403
www.balboapress.com
1-(877) 407-4847

ISBN: 978-1-4525-7329-8 (sc)
ISBN: 978-1-4525-7330-4 (e)

Library of Congress Control Number: 2013907462

Printed in the United States of America.

Balboa Press rev. date: 06/21/2019

BALBOA.
PRESS
A DIVISION OF HAY HOUSE

About the Author:

Debbie Lindsay is a Holistic Life Coach in Gilbert, AZ and is the Executive Director of High Joy Enterprises, LLC. She has dedicated many years in assisting people of all ages in achieving physical, emotional, mental and spiritual wellbeing.

Debbie married her high school sweetheart, Curtis Lindsay, on December 29, 1982. They have three grown daughters: Danielle, Lacey Jo and BrieAnn and three amazing son-in-laws Chris, Travis and Andrew with eight grandchildren total (and possibly more on the way).

About the Illustrator:

Francois Lange was born in Paris, France. He has been drawing since he was very little.

His first drawings were and continue to be his best friends.

Francois has worked in the animation industry and currently works as an illustrator in sunny Florida.

He has a very successful virtual sketchbook online that he blissfully decorates daily with his sketches to celebrate the joy of simply being in the present moment. Visit him at: Sketchesinstillness.com.

Debbie and Francois are forever grateful for having been guided by the universe to write and illustrate this beautiful children's book together. Such an experience has truly been the fruitage of their intention to be an instrument through word and art, for bringing peace and joy in any way possible to children all around the world.

A special thank you to layout designer, Matthew Jorgensen for seeing and matching our vision and bringing all the elements together so perfectly.

Jordin is a girl with a very special skill.

JORDIN JUGGLES!

Balls and beanbags, pencils and pens,

they all go flying when Jordin walks in.

Wiggling, jiggling, and even giggling,

Jordin juggles without end.

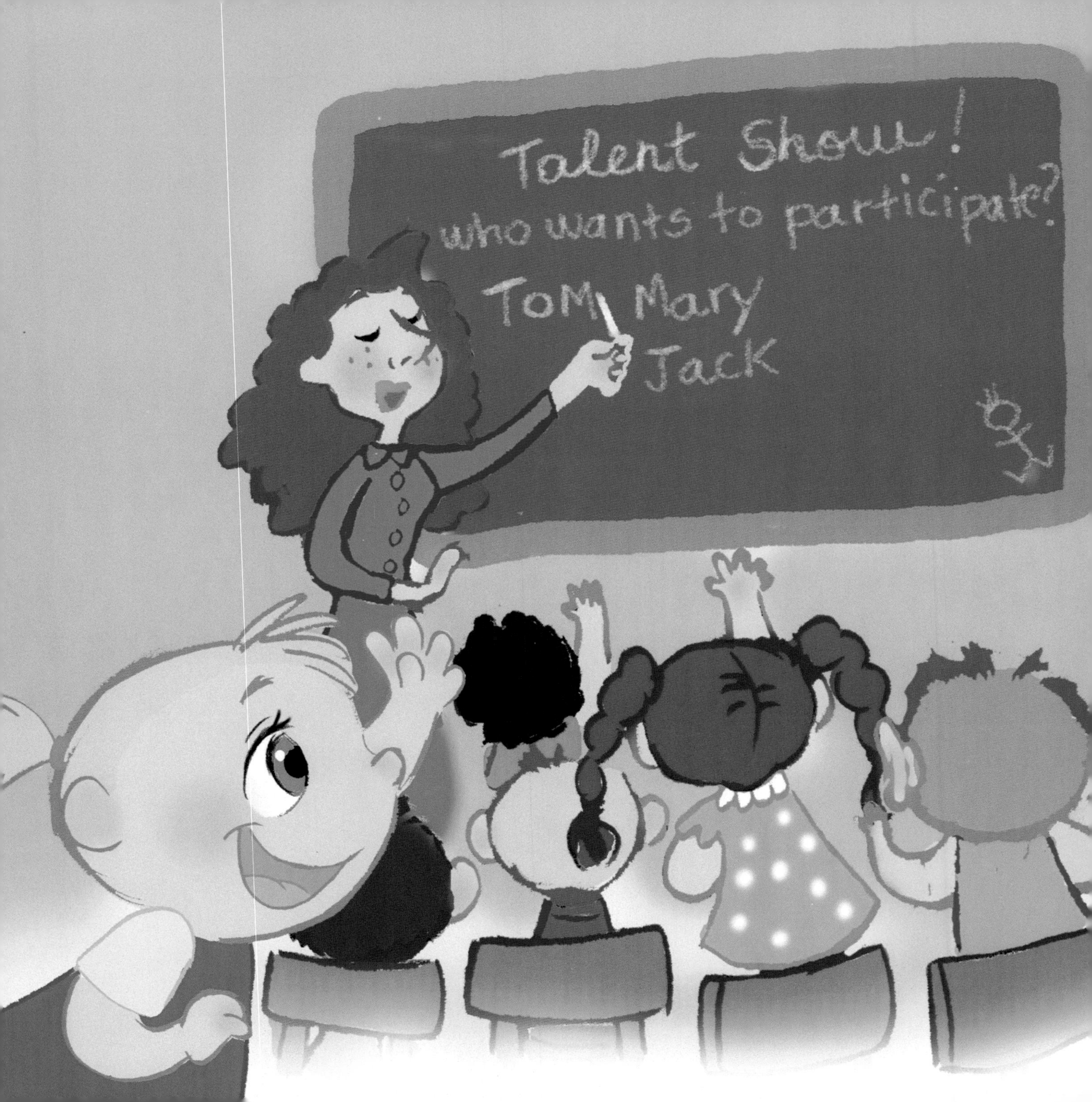
Talent Show!
who wants to participate?
ToM Mary
Jack

Every year her school puts on a talent show. Jordin wants to be in the show but she is a little afraid. Row after row of kids will watch her on stage. What if she stumbles or fumbles that day?

"What if I stumble"

Oh, how FEAR juggles Jordin's mind!

Jordin makes an orange outfit with giant bright buttons. Then she bakes cupcakes in row after row. She will juggle the cupcakes!

WOW, WHAT A SHOW!

But FEAR is still there. FEAR haunts her mind. If only she could leave FEAR far behind.

Jordin goes to school to practice her act. The stage seems so big and she feels so small. The spotlight shines right in her eyes. Jordin tosses the cupcakes but can't catch a one.

They land all around her and on her.
Her moves are all wrong!

Jordin storms off the stage. She has left FEAR behind but now here comes RAGE! She is covered in frosting and cupcake crumbs. She is mad at the spotlight and that big, lonely stage. She is mad at the cupcakes and the mess that they made.

Most of all,
Jordin is mad
at herself.

The moment Jordin gets home, she runs to her room. What else can she do? Her act is doomed! She must not be a juggler after all, not a wiggler or a jiggler, and never a giggler! Here comes SADNESS, an awful lump. Jordin juggles nothing but tears.

For the longest time, Jordin sits all alone. Her thoughts are a clanging, calamitous mess. They tease her and taunt her and bring back that FEAR. Then ANGER jumps in with SADNESS still near. The trio is terrible, awful and mean. They spin in her head like a tornado team!

Jordin feels dizzy from all of that whirling. The tornado team tries really hard to make her feel sickly. They are very small yet they seem so wicked.

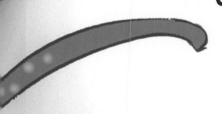

They are itty and bitty

and just plain icky. They are the

Itty Bitty Icky Committee!

Jordin turns off the light to drive them away.

You'll never be good enough!
Give up! they say.

She thinks of the spotlight back on the stage.

It shone so bright like a summery day.

What if that LIGHT
could drive them away?

She turns on her lamp
and points it at FEAR.

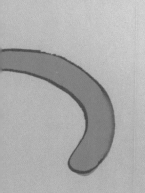

Poof!

He'sgone!

RAGE and SADNESS are on the run.

Jordin aims that lamp like a ray gun!

RAGE is next to whither and die.

SADNESS is caught in the corner.

BYE-BYE!

The Itty Bitty Icky Committee is no more. Darkness and bad thoughts can't live in the LIGHT!

Jordin grabs her dolls and stuffed toys. She juggles and jiggles. She even giggles! Whenever a bad thought creeps back in, she imagines that light is inside her head. Her spotlight is strong, it's white and it's warm. With a flip of the switch, that bright light comes on!

Jordin decides to be in that show. She'll wiggle and jiggle, and maybe she'll win. The Itty Bitty Icky Committee can't stop her now. If they try, she'll just zap them! Oh, how that spotlight shines in her head. A flip of the switch.

"How simple,"

she says.

Flip the Book and Flip Your Switch!

Inside her head, the spotlight shines as bright as the sun.

Now the show's over. Jordin's parents take her home. The Heroes of the Heart spin gently nearby. Their whirling is never an icky tornado. Jordin feels so happy and good. Her act was great and she had lots of fun.

Jordin's chest flutters again. The Heroes of the Heart are spinning in there. JOY lets her know that she did her best. HOPE whispers that she might win next year. Best of all is Love's special touch. She loves her friend Taggert and also herself.

The Itty Bitty Icky Committee never gave her that much!

It's Taggert, of course,
with his big pogo stick!

Who will win?
Who was the best?

It's time for the judges to add up the score. Backstage, the kids wait and then wait some more. Finally they are called out together. They fidget and fuss, they blush and they chatter.

Taggert is next with his big pogo stick. He bounces and pops and spins while he hops. Right at the end, he does a full flip! When he lands on his feet, the kids stand and shout. Jordin claps with them. Taggert's the best! His act is much better than all of the rest!

Jordin takes a bow before leaving the stage. She isn't alone, no not anymore. High overhead is a brand new committee. HOPE, LOVE and JOY fly like kites on the wind. They are the Heroes of the Heart.

What a great prize to win!

The kids all go crazy!

Jordin finally steps onto the stage.
She tosses and catches, she
spins and she jumps. She juggles
those cupcakes so high it's amazing!
And for her finale, she throws the
cupcakes one more time. They land
in a stack.

Jordin buttons her costume up to her chin. She's so happy to be in the show. Winning and ribbons really don't matter.

The JOY that fills her is oh, so much better!

It's the best of the best, the brightest of bright. She will juggle and jiggle with all of her might!

She flips on the spotlight
and drives it away!

Jordin goes backstage to help set up for the show.

As she moves the props and the scenery around,

she finds one tiny thing that makes her frown.

It's a smear of frosting from that awful, bad day.

SADNESS swoops down to tap on her chest.

Jordin's friend Taggert has watched her juggle plenty of times. Her act has even made him giggle! He can't wait to see her jiggle and wiggle. She feels so good talking to him. He really is a special friend. And what is that overhead? It's LOVE floating on a gentle wind!

She flips that switch and beams out bright light.

The Itty Bitty Icky Committee dare not come near!

At lunch Jordin flies down the hall. She doesn't feel worried, no, not at all. Then two girls talk about that awful day on that big, empty stage. They laugh and they roar and then talk some more. RAGE whirls in and tickles Jordin's ear.

While sitting in class, Jordin feels great. Her act will astound all of her friends. She'll toss those cupcakes wide and high. She'll spin and prance and juggle and dance! She feels a flutter in her chest that's quite nice. The flutter must be HOPE. That's much better than fright!

Juggling Jordin wakes up happy. Today is the talent show! She has a pretty orange outfit and cupcakes galore. She'll jiggle and wiggle and juggle them all! FEAR tries to chill her but she puts up a fight. She just flips the switch on her inner spotlight.

Zap!
FEAR disappears!

Balboa Press books may be ordered through booksellers or by contacting:

Balboa Press
A Division of Hay House
1663 Liberty Drive
Bloomington, IN 47403
www.balboapress.com
1-(877) 407-4847

ISBN: 978-1-4525-7329-8 (sc)
ISBN: 978-1-4525-7330-4 (e)

Library of Congress Control Number: 2013907462

Printed in the United States of America.

Balboa Press rev. date: 06/21/2019

BALBOA
PRESS
A DIVISION OF HAY HOUSE

Printed in the United States
By Bookmasters